AUTUMN ROAD

2/22

AUTUMN ROAD

Brian Swann

THE OHIO STATE UNIVERSITY PRESS • COLUMBUS

Library of Congress Cataloging-in-Publication Data

Swann, Brian.
    Autumn road / Brian Swann.
        p. cm.
    ISBN 0-8142-1012-0 (alk. Paper) — ISBN 0-8142-5147-1 (pbk.: alk. Paper) —
    ISBN 0-8142-9090-6 (cd-rom)
        I. Title.
    PS3569.W256A97 2005
    811'.54—dc22
                            2005006676

Cover design by Dan O'Dair
Cover painting by Brian Swann
Typesetting by Malcolm Litchfield
Printed by McNaughton Gunn, Inc.

The paper used in this publication meets the minimum requirements of the
American National Standard for Information Sciences—Permanence of Paper
for Printed Library Materials. ANSI Z39.48–1992.

9   8   7   6   5   4   3   2   1

FOR MY DEAR WIFE ROBERTA

"Everything happens suddenly,
No matter how long it takes."

CONTENTS

Credits

1 THE LOST BOY

2 ARS AMATORIA

3   ESCHATOLOGY

CREDITS

The poems in the following list originally appeared in the publications indicated.

Agni: Dis Pater
American Scholar: Rain of the Waldensians
Anthropology and Humanism: Slugs; Soft Boiled Eggs
Chicago Review: Heliography
Conjunctions: Orderly
Crazyhorse: More; The Psychoanalysis of Fire
Harvard Review: Amsterdam
Hotel Amerika: The Rose
Iowa Review: The Skull; Three Score and Then Some
Metre (Great Britain): De Profundis
New Republic: Calendar Girl; The Wind and the Rain; Rain
North American Review: The Painting
Notre Dame Review: Shadows and Distance; Fens; Eschatology; The Wanderer
Paris Review: Consumed; Alzheimer's; Exist
Partisan Review: Neruda in Purgatory; The Lost Boy
Ploughshares: The Star
Poetry: The Point; Habeas Corpus; Painting by Anon; The Economy of Windmills
Poetry Northwest: Where the Woods Begin; Ars Amatoria
Prairie Schooner: Basso-Relievo
Prism International (Canada): Birdnesting; Catch; Watch Yourself
Quarterly Review of Literature: Variations on the First Elegy
Raritan: Le Grand Mal
Stand (Great Britain): Quasar; My Aunt
TriQuarterly: Deep Fish; Inspiration
Yale Review: Whiteness; HIV; Physics; Somewhere

THE LOST BOY

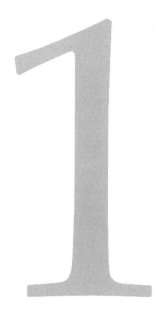

HELIOGRAPHY

Mæg ic be me sylfum   soðgied wrecan.
— "The Seafarer"

Losing I can accept,   a long process like mould.
That way I got to know this place   in another way,
like seeing the Pleiades   from the other side.
It could have been worse, I suppose.   I could
never have been here,   instead of having been flung
headlong into whatever it is,   light breaking over me
and fingertips reaching at me,   the old fat guide
picking me up. I'm your granny,   she said. And
your mammy, and your pappy,   god rest his whatever.
I will call you by your initial letter   and you will
live with me catty-corner.   You will eat your fingerprints
in silence, and everything   will resolve itself as if
a plot. She took me home   where keyholes made my eyes
lengthen and shrink until soon   it was time to leave.
They called it dead-man-time.   The prostitutes who had
taken me everywhere with them   spat the last seeds
into my mouth and sent me   on my way. They tasted
of seasons and the wild   gyrations of atoms. Conjecture,
introversion, wild surmise had   made up my world.
Now I needed new illusions.   Soon I was making up
my lives and the lives of others,   biographies to live
for themselves but in me   till I was full of inventories,
full of mirrors and ventriloquisms,   and a rusty angel
who faked his face but never   opened his mail, who
slept on the windowsill suspecting   rebuffs from every
angle, and who collided regularly   at take-off with
the same tree. But as for me   I grew a colon for eyes
and bells for ears. Shaken foil   was my trust, the Zodiac
my toy. So here I am, in a   parole of flowers, flapping
through libraries, outmoded,   outmatched, but not yet
old enough to be my own ghost.   So I place these ghosts
on paper, anonymous, ambiguous,   festive as a crowd
in an unnoticed world,   myself a character who will not

rehearse any more, determined still   to be someone similar to
who I am, but not me, keeping at it,   mistaking the sky for
something else, mistaking flashes   from my fingers for heliography!

VAULT

August 1940, Leo rising somewhere
   in the night, the Nile's flood rising,
fountains flowing somewhere else
   while here rain has held off
where a birth has made another echo
   in this house. The stars straighten themselves out
as an airraid siren swirls like a dragon's tail.
   A dice is thrown. Overhead, caught in
brilliant crosshairs, something waits
   for the ack-ack, falls like Lucifer.
I come spinning out, space still in my eyes,
   then take off through the open window
scarcely looking back. People
   disappear, towns dwindle. As they look
for something to aim at they can see me
   against the sky, pulling on my ice-skin,
spreading out my tail, squatting down in Leo
   until it runs out, spiraling down the sky.
Rain coughs, sputters, carries me
   back down, wheeling about like a sycamore seed,
over fields, over raspberries gleaming
   like fresh menstrual blood, drifting in
an open window where a woman
   is lying on her back, face to one side,
emptiness inside her vaulted with constellations
   like an Egyptian tomb with a great woman
spread across it wall to wall.

INSPIRATION
(on being asked)

Each day I've climbed up here
and faced down the leaves and buds
pushing at my window, or looked
down on white pines whirling in
their fibonacci dance. And each day
I've felt like stone, or a stone
in my mouth, or at the tip of
each finger; hidebound when I
wanted to be endless. So today
I again try being endless. No luck.
I've no idea how it feels, or how
to start. Maybe I need a crisis like
sitting on a railing, OK, a fence,
overlooking a deep gully, about
to collapse, forcing me to jump.
I jump. I snap my neck. Crisis over.
End of story. Time for a break.
But no. I'm lucky. The fence
has led me to an old porch and
rocking-chair. The war's over,
but my father's still away at sea.
I don't know him. He hasn't yet
pulled us up and moved us south.
There's a meerschaum clamped
in my grandfather's mouth.
In one hand's the ounce of twist
he sent me for, and in the other
a pearl-hafted penknife to slice it with.
There's his smoke mingling with
the smoke of house fires, and maybe there's
the lingering smell of fires still smouldering
underground. From here it's a small step
to the dawntime tramp of miners
changing shifts down cobbled lanes,
to and from the Rising Sun. It all stops
a few days a year for the pitmen's holiday
and fair where they put their hobnail boots

to better use, kicking the living daylights
out of each other for more money
than they could make in a month.
That's me watching all this,
the sloshing pints, giggling girls and
women old at thirty. I've come up
to Ashington in my uncle's charabanc
on what they call a "mystery tour"
though everyone knows where
they're going. That's me on the way home,
stopping at Rowland's Gill so I can
throw up, and cousin Neil can fall
into the stream. That's me stripped
by mother and grandmother
to supply clothes, protesting, until
"Hit him, Neil. He's a cissy," and
a fight breaks out. And that's my
Auntie Violet in the front seat, maybe
a little tipsy on sloe gin, letting out
a shriek and pointing out the window:
"Ee—look! They're doing it! In the field!"
"Whisht, woman! There's bairns here!"—
Uncle Len. As if we didn't know all
there was to know, we who'd put feathers
to uses that were never intended, making
headdresses for where there were no heads
(imagine, reader). We to whom Molly Oates,
crouched down under cover of Queen Anne's lace
and elder bushes, had shown what
she'd learned from *Married Love,* what
was what and who went where, the day the soil
beneath our feet turned red and we ran home,
hell at our heels, slap into Michael Dunleavy
running the other way, a pack of mothers
yelling at his heels, and him shouting: "Come
and watch the cows being fucked!
Come and watch the cows being fucked!"
So we turned round and ran with him.
Hell could wait.

GRANDPARENTS

Boots, black boots he always wears, whether down the garden path
    and off to the "The Winning" or "The Coach and Horses," or even,
it seemed possible, wearing them to bed where, as my grandmother
    informs me, aged eight, "he likes his bit o'tail." He keeps them bright
as his wartime Special Constable uniform buttons and pin, spit aimed
    precisely on stiff toecaps, blacking poised on finger-tented rag.
As he rubs and spits they turn to mirrors where I can see
    the second him, bald and busy, mustachioed and bald.
He is always doing something after he retired as Head Geeker at the G Pit
    and the Rising Sun, inspector of bituminous coal that made the town
and blighted the landscape, sometimes turning earth the color
    of dry blood when fires burn underground and make the cows
nervous as I drive them down to the Burn Closes. They take off,
    and in the evening when I drive them back up, they try
to find a way around, but can't, and gallop up Burn Bank,
    across the Village Green, straight into the milking barn at
Johnny Woodgett's farm. In the dairy, cool with water that
    drips down moss-covered walls, I ladle unpasteurized milk
from churn to bottle, popping the cardboard cap on each.
    With Toby in the shafts, Mr. Long at the reins, I leave
the morning milk on doorsteps. Granda never touches the stuff.
    His milk is Newcastle Brown which he sips while rolling up
a sleeve. When done, he injects himself with insulin and drops
    the empty vial to the floor of the shed he'd built at garden's end,
out of sight from the house. We share the place with Dick,
    the ex–pit pony who nips my backside each time I push by
in quarters cramped with dog and cat, ducks that lay Granda's favorite

                                                   eggs,

    strong and blue as heaven, hens and yellow chicks he'd hatched
beside the coal-stove. Dick earns his keep on Sundays, pulling
    a two-wheeled trap that takes the three of us through town
in our best clothes. The rest of the week he wheezes as Granda smokes
    his twist and spits into the fire. I spit too, from the pipe he carved me.
Down here, we all escape Nanna's tongue and chores, especially
    the Monday wash that always got her all worked up in the wash-house
where she'd hosed me down more than once after I ran home with
    my pants full, refusing to use the open outdoor toilets at our school.
While the whole place steams, she goes at the tub with her poss-stick,

squeezing the clothes flat in the mangle, then attacking the
clothes-line with the pole as if she meant to vault it, tossing it up
triumphant, spare wooden clothespegs in her mouth like fangs.
Then from the line blossom pink camiknickers, voluminous bloomers,
huge brassieres, shirts, blouses, longjohns, sheets and pillowcases,
socks and skirts and trousers. Once she dropped everything to join
the women chasing nine-year-old Michael Dunleavy running
down the street yelling "Come and watch the cows being fucked!"
forgetting she had clothespegs in her mouth, and almost choked.
When Granda and I aren't in the shed smoking, or sucking
his sweet black bullets, big as doorknobs, or cleaning harness, he
tells stories of pit disasters, his time as air-raid warden, the launching
of the *Mauritania* in '06, or how he'd walked ten miles each way
from Wallsend to Benton each night to woo my grandmother.
Many days we hunker down over red bricks, smashing them to bits
for the path that runs around the rockery that doubled as air-raid shelter
my first five years, under trellises, through flowerbeds, past chicken-coop
and garden-shed, beside the lawn and, if he hadn't died, it would probably
have gone up the house and over the slate roof with shrapnel shards
still embedded in the eaves. But I see him now on the sofa, after dinner,
reaching up over his head, wedging a slice of apple between the bars
                                                                    beside
a hunk of cheese, while the canary, saved from the pits, sings his thanks,
and Granda's favorite hymn, "Abide With Me," plays from the radio.
And I see Nanna, day's work done, in her bedroom, loosening
her corset, unsnapping the thick leather belt with knobbed ends
big as fists that hold her insides in after six kids. Standing in front
of the dresser mirror she stares at herself. Then tosses belt and corset
onto the bed where they land beneath a sepia photo on the wall
of a two-wheel trap and a pony, new-shod by her father, the blacksmith.
They share a blanket over their laps. She's sporting a beribboned boater,
holding a thin whip in her right hand, reins lightly in her left.
Granda wears a trilby at an angle. In black ink, corner right, her script:
Benton, 1900. The photo on my desk.

In memoriam, James and Elizabeth Booth

THE PAINTING

The music I sat on, in long rolls, you stuck
them in, pushed pedals with your feet, &
under your fingers watched the keys go up & down
& the rolls go round & round, the notes following
the holes, in the front parlor where no one went
but no dust settled on the wax flowers on
the mahogany sideboard or covered sofa & chairs,
or the leaded windows with roses diamonds & lozenges
in deep colors so when the sun shone you were
in them, reds & greens, blues & golds staining
your skin so when you played the pianola the sounds
came out colored & took you away—
"Custer's Last Stand" was golds & reds, "Old Folks
at Home" blues & greens & yellows, all the songs
my Aunt Violet loved like "Hear My Song" were blue,
tailing off into a color I could not name. You could
hide in that room & no one would ever find you
if you kept quiet. You could roll wax petals into
little balls or make new petals & stick them
onto other stalks & no one would notice. It was
a room whose importance was just being there,
useful for not being used. Everybody crammed into
the kitchen, along with the dog, cat, canary, skittering
yellow chicks just hatched in the warm place beside
the fire. But there was another room next to the parlor
which we decorated with paper bells at Christmas
& then forgot. There was a painting in this room
that took up almost one wall. Twice a year, my grandma
and I spread newspaper over the heavy table never used
for anything else, placed on it small brushes & pots
of gold paint & carefully repainted the huge carved
gold frame. This only seemed to make the painting darker
& recede deeper. Already, it was so dark you could
hardly make out anything. But there were a lot of
massive trees like none I'd ever seen that overhung
a deep black pool in the mountains. Someone was
down there, standing on an overhanging rock, staring off
into what distance there was left, & pointing. There were

10

almost no colors, like evening. I used to creep into that room
as often as I dared to look at that painting. Sometimes
I felt I could climb into it like through a window &
into a life far away that seemed to go on forever
& that was already mine if only I knew where.

THE SKULL

I'd dug it from the pit, thinking it a fossil.
I'd cleaned it up & held it upside-down
in one hand where it felt like my own head.
There was no jaw. We looked everywhere.
I set him up on a lump of chalk, gave him
a tongue & made him talk, telling me
about his life, but Derek shut me up.
Maybe it's worth something, he said.
So we brought it in & showed it to
our History teacher, Mr. Barlow, who had
just been talking to us about the Devil's Dike
& Wandlebury, Beaker Folk, the local
Bronze Age & other stuff that set me dreaming.
He said to take the skull to the Museum
of Arch & Eth, & that was where we learned
it was an Anglo-Saxon boy about our age,
but older by about a thousand years.
He must have lived up there on top of what
were now abandoned chalk pits, doing what
boys do, playing with his brothers & his friends,
maybe even finding the very fossils that brought me
so often to this place after school, scrambling
through the rubble at the foot of cliffs,
filling pockets with ammonites & snails, chitons
& cephalopods. Perhaps he found them too,
but didn't know what they were, calling them
"dragon's teeth," or "stone flowers," & took them
back to his hut to share, but then forgot about,
so maybe some of those he picked were hidden
in my own collection under shirts & underwear
until my father found them & dumped them out.
"If you spent more time on useful things, like mathematics,"
he said, "you'd be better off. You can't do anything.
You'll end up as a dustman. You'll end up on the streets."
I tried to say that history's useful too. *Shut up,*
he said. *Like talking to a brick wall. Numbskull.*
And he hit me on the head. I thought about
that boy a lot, up there, all alone, abandoned,

not buried in one of those cemeteries we'd read about
with gravegoods & relatives & sometimes a horse
or dog or two. What was on his mind? Did no one
miss him when he didn't come home that evening?
If they did, did they go out to look for him
on that windswept heath, calling his name?
He could have been an ancestor of mine, sort of.
How did he die? Maybe he killed himself, or someone
killed him. Maybe he got lost, got water in his lungs
from falling in a fen so he couldn't breathe or speak,
like my friend Alf whose lungs collapsed & whose head
was long, like his. What did he see out those sockets
as he looked over to where our streets would be,
our school, & where his skull would end up on a shelf
in the basement of the university's Museum of Archeology and Ethnology,
growing even more silent with the years, in a box with other skulls,
above which, years later, on my first day as a freshman
I would sit with three others in a large room around a huge
oak table as white-haired Dr. Whitelock came in & greeted us,
then turned to me & said: "Please open your copy of *Beowulf*
to page one, and start translating." *Hwaet!* I could. I did, until she said,
"Thank you. Very good. Stop now. Next." But no one really could.
After class, Jenny Daiches invited me to her rooms. I couldn't go.
I'd discovered that what you came to learn here, you were already supposed
                                                                              to know.

PHYSICS

"This grand book of the universe . . . is written in the language of mathematics."
—Galileo

Under windows, boxes of polished brass and glass.
Inside, carefully balanced dust-proof scales &
below, in neat rows, brass weights like buttons,
arranged by size up & down the wooden floor.
Light caught inside bounced around unable to be measured,
at least by me though the promise was it could be if only
I could get the laws Mr. Bulman wrote on the board
day after day which everyone else got but
the only way I could was to copy their homework
which led to the deepest recesses of dark deceit.
So I sat in place, moving my head just a little at
a time to avoid detection & detention, up down all around
so everything flowed into everything else & the spectrum
split instead of staying still until the boxes
disappeared & everything in them into a gleam that turned
the sill to shining & everything on it & I knew
enough to know it all ended in my eyes (optics)
but from there, who knows, maybe it flew back out
to illuminate like headlights what had illuminated it
(guesswork) & this was how we knew the world
& maybe all the light that ever was had already been
in my eyes & out again, like the air everyone had breathed
since the start of time but which was still there,
so I swam in this element until the bell went
& we were dismissed into remaining light that had,
at one time or another, been us & we it, even though
now it was all mixed up with all sorts of other stuff,
and that was the way things were.

SLUGS

Who could have dreamed them up? At least snails
have shells, but all these have is—nothing.
Small black antennae like fat pins wave
as if they could take in enough to get them through.
Turn them over, they're the soles of new shoes,
pale and unmarked as babies. They flow,
the soil itself learning how to move and, moving,
almost staying still, their silver monorail
the only evidence of where they'd been.
And they die quiet, or at least (thankfully)
out of the human ear's range, between two stones,
under heels, shriveling in salt or piss, at the tips
of sharp sticks. Fight back, I hear myself say,
do *something*. Don't just take it. But they die
as they had lived, exuding slime, like
the smaller boys, who'd just
stand there, miserable in short pants,
school socks down to their ankles,
school tie unknotted and askew, and flowing
from noses slow cauls of snot that
from time to time they'd lick or sniff back up
part way, until it flowed again, coating
the upper lip, falling into the mouth, mixing
with tears before anything had been done,
the fear itself enough, so even if we wanted
we couldn't let them off. Sometimes it was
the knee "where you daren't show your mother,"
other times the kick in the shins, the stick over
the head, the punch in the mouth, while they
just stood there, or double up, gasping
for breath, and we did it again.

THE LOST BOY

per me si va tra la perdutta gente.

Different, in darkness, the twig was bent back
down into the ground. So it will grow. Paterpornographer
warmed the child in his hand, producing a crop

of continuing silence, prison with small sky. The robber
of the name still shares the name that opens
its night in night, secret tainted flower,

while in the interlocking circles, action
has retreated to the depth of decades where
love's first star's still propped up in

its empty blue. So whenever something near
shines the boy-man closes his face, quickly turns away
from more than rumors on the wind, from far

back, speaking evacuated houses, dues paid
in blood. Now through the rusty drizzle of chrysanthemums
he hears a drumming from where water pools, delayed,

slips through rocks, over the abandoned road, runs
through the dead yew's roots into the orchard where
over-ripe apples still hang, and the nightly procession's left some

scraps and shreds like shadows caught there
on bushes, stirring when a lost child passes,
a breath inside the ghost, hanging here,

the fruit of nightmare, picked again by hands that catch
at, grope, suborn, *a fantasy come home,*
forever he's leaving his own life, fast

and faster, man-child impaled on the shrike's thorn
of his own mind, hearing voices of women
fainter, half-light wrapped loose around them.

While on horseback, painted phallus with eyes strapped on,
the father still gathers him for distances
cranes know, making long streaks of themselves in

air. *It's not wrong.* Kept a child. That voice professes
everything unchanged, praises the "natural";
via parody, everything's a dance, of weariness;

that authority in the very waves' back-curl's
always about to swamp his little boat
with innuendoed intimacies. The call

of a wild dog limps away. Silence bloats.

SOFT BOILED EGGS

"Spirits clothe themselves with all things of man's memories."
—Swedenborg

Brachycephalic, dolichocephalic, it was hard to tell.
  I had to know, but everything changes if you look
too close, like when I tried to see if I really had
  a Greek or Roman nose by standing sideways to the mirror
and straining eyeballs left or right, or walking down the street
  and closing one eye to squint inward with the other.
Each time I saw a hump-back conk, a nose with a hillock
  in the middle I didn't want and would have liked
to obey the injunction to pluck it from my face
  the way I plucked raw the sparse to nonexistent brows
between my eyes because my dad said they met,
  which showed I was deceitful. I couldn't tell from photos
if my head was wide or long. Where was I from?
  I kept consulting *The Races of Britain* (1898),
borrowed from Heffer's Bookshop where I worked one summer,
  during which I sold a Selected Tennyson to Benjamin Britten
in from Aldeburgh with Peter Pears, and so I was responsible
  in part for the "Nocturne" suite I love: "The splendor falls/on castle
                                                                    walls."
He was, I'd say, dolichocephalic, though Pears—I wasn't sure.
  Same for James Frazer, whom I'd just discovered,
and whose copy of Lady Guest's *Mabinogion* I had bought
  for sixpence from the outside stall with "J.G.Frazer, Trinity College,
1906" on the inside cover. I read his *Golden Bough*
  with its dying vegetation gods, among whom he couldn't quite
bring himself to say Christ was one, and its killing of the sacred king,
  spending my lunch hours cross-legged on the balcony
that ran around and above the shop, finishing all ten volumes.
  And when I'd finished them, Swedenborg's *Compendium* (1875)
whose Moon spirits danced down, piggybank, with faces "longer than
  the faces of other spirits" (like Swedenborg himself),
and "not unhandsome," and spirits of the planet Mars
  with whom he was "instantly friends," who associated with
congenial minds, and knew it instantly by the *face.*
  Up on the virtually deserted balcony, a virtual virgin,

I wished to become one of those most excellent spirits
    and angels of Jupiter who went naked because they lived
in a state of innocence, and I tried to imagine all those
    beneath me I saw through the railings, interrupting
my reading, especially the women and girls, all of us
    in a state of innocence, like naked Blake and his wife
in their Hampstead garden. At home, hours of mirror-gazing,
    trying to decide once and for all the length of my head,
I realized my dad was right (if he was my dad). My lips
    were too sensuous and wide. I tried to tone them down
by reducing the muscles through silence, though those
    excellent Jupiter spirits had faces "prominent about the lips,"
caused by speech unrestrained sent forth freely. Actually
    I never spoke much anyway, especially with my father present.
My mother, whose explanation for everything was "jealousy,"
    fed me breakfast after he'd left and dinner before he returned.
Unlike among the Jupiter spirits, there were no long meals
    for pleasure of conversation, sitting on fig-leaves, eating
wholesole food. "Alpine," "Nordic," "Mediterranean,"
    I sorted through subdivisions, drawings of skulls and heads,
maps of Europe in different colors, measurements, ratios,
    tables, and even learned the cephalic index (B divided by L
times 100) though couldn't use it. I looked about for
    history in the present. Winston Churchill was clearly an
Iron Age intruder, Belgic, and my friend Alf a Teuton,
    although brown-haired. Teutons were thin and Alf was thin
as the cricket bat he loved. He'd not yet suffered
    the collapsed lung that made him thinner just before the college
scholarship exams, but his asthma and constant catarrh
    that kept him muffled were on the TB road probably caused
by his long-headed Angle ancestors sitting in mud,
    though more likely by his bricklayer father from Lowestoft
who refused him heat and light so he had either to do
    his homework with the family huddled round the TV or
wrap himself in blankets in the bedroom he shared
    with his brother and suffer the blasts from fen winds unfettered
from the Urals. Alf had a good head, the mind shining through
    like a good Jupiterian and a long narrow face which, however,
a Jupiter spirit might not have found attractive because they
    found "deformed" anything with pimples. Alf was a clear case,

but you had to pay close attention because other schoolmates,
   especially those from the fens, also had long and narrow faces,
but with black hair and dark eyes. Smallish, wiry, they were
   Iberian aborigines, origin of fairy-folk, like the Fir Bolg
in Ireland displaced into hiding by the fairhaired Tuatha de Danaan.
   In their fastnesses of Quy, Ely, Manea, Whittlesea, and other islands
now drained to the dry name of islands they held out against
all invaders. They were exotic, sly, a bit primitive, like the farmer
a nurse told me of who came in complaining of a tickling in his foot
   that was swathed in a filthy bandage. He'd put a pitchfork
through it. When? Some ten years back. She cut the cloth
   to find a green and wormy stump. So, I knew what I wasn't,
but the only real clue I had to what I was was my fair hair,
   the best kind, and a tooth like Sven Bluetooth and a name
that could be Sven, or plain peasant, or a bird-name derived
   from the Sanskrit for "sound," or just plain "pig-keeper," which
wasn't all that bad since I'd learned from Robert Graves
   the sacredness of swine, and their dedication to the Mother Goddess
(carved tusks and crescent moons). But all this was not
   enough for clarity. Fair hair and blue eyes. Brown eyes meant
black blood somewhere in the family tree. Sometimes I
   wished I had some. My father said they were a happy people.
He knew them well from his time on the West Indies Station
   before the War (a war he fought honorably mostly in the
North Atlantic, and was decorated, though he said we should
   have fought the Frogs and Ruskies. Germans were our brothers).
"I got on well with niggers. A happy people. They'd laugh
   even if their arses were on fire." I had one big nostril, African
almost. My dad said their nostrils were that way because
   of the heat while Nordics had narrow nostrils to warm the cold air.
I tried to keep the big nostril away from anyone I was talking to,
   so I always seemed to be looking into the distance. And my cheekbones
were a clue though I didn't know to what. I didn't seem
   to have any. Maybe just as well. My dad said Asiatics got
high cheekbones from living on the steppes and pressing
   their faces hard against the flanks of mares at milking.
Both my mother's parents had had black hair, though
   granda was bald when I came along. His family was from Cumberland,
land of the Cymri, or Welsh, medieval Rheged. My grandmother's
   family came from Norfolk. What were black-haired folk doing

in Norfolk? Perhaps an enclave of the Celts. But Caesar said
   the Celts were blond or red of hair, like Boudicca. It must have been
those Iberians again. The quest continued, though now,
   having stumbled over Jung, I added the task of finding out if I
was extrovert or introvert. The latter was clearly superior.
   Alf was introvert, and I was just as shy as he, maybe
more secretive, poring over Freud's *Totem and Taboo*
   at night in my room where the primal hoard of sons did in
their dad (a rotten bugger anyway). But would an introvert
   have hit his dad so hard he staggered backwards hanging onto me
via the sweater my mother had just knitted and I was wearing
   for the first time so he fell backwards into a chair dragging me
down on top of him while he tore the wool to shreds and
   I let him? Maybe. But maybe too an extrovert would have
killed him. A real introvert was sensitive, like Alf, singing
   nasal versions of Sinatra love-songs to the air. An introvert
could stand staring straight ahead thinking thoughts that
   lie too deep for words. Actually, you never knew what
he was thinking, or maybe, like spirits, his language consisted
   of ideas in place of words and sounds so an introvert could
easily be confused with somebody who plotted to deceive
   or plain didn't care. Keats, my favorite poet, in his vale
of soulmaking, was clearly introvert. The braggart Byron,
   not. Shelley maybe, Wordsworth too, but not the cynical Augustans.
The early Yeats, the later not, the public man. I learned
   a lot of him by heart for use with girls. Introverts were attractive
to girls. I wanted to be an introvert because on a caravan
   vacation in Kessingland I'd fallen for one Sylvia Jones (blonde)
and her friend Janet Jones (black). Both were older than me,
   eighteen, women. Janet's father was the Rev. Owen Jones
of the BBC's "Lift Up Your Hearts," from Bangor (Gwynedd).
   I loved them both, but Sylvia maybe more. I wrote "I Love
Sylvia Jones" on steam on our kitchen window and my mother
   saw it before I could wipe it off. I kept a cut-out ad of
the Hovis girl, a dead ringer, inside my bedside drawer.
   When my father found it I protested the invasion of my privacy,
but he said it was his house and I shouldn't have secrets.
   But Janet Jones was even more alluring. She had black hairs
on her big toes, and pagan eyes, full of nocturnal mystery,
   like Eustacia Vye, and told dirty jokes like, "If a broad bean

is a single-decker bus, and a runner bean is a single-decker,
what's a pea? Give up? A Relief!" The following summer, when I took
a day off from camp in Benllech, North Wales, I visited her.

Her mother served soft-boiled eggs for lunch, dolichocephalic.

THE WAR

That's us, coating our clogs with candlewax &
sliding before school in front of the open latrines.
That's us peeling off pullovers, jerkins, jumpers,
so underneath thin shirts newspapers & butcher's paper flap out,
or the thick brown sheets Jenny used to wrap warm bread in
from her shop. And that's us being herded into assembly
& everybody singing "Oh hear us when we cry to Thee/
For those in peril on the sea," which accounts for
more than half our dads. At break, we join a line,
any line, not knowing what is at the end, a bun,
an Oxo cube, a piece of orange peel, something
we've never seen before & don't know what to do with,
& so we eat it. Then back to sums & stories &
tossing beanbags up & catching on the fly in circles
so we can't stop. And when the sea replies to all
our hymns & our fathers, some of them, come home,
there are flags, balloons, & parties that run up & down
our cobbled lanes & streets, tables & benches set out like
harvest home. That's when the clocks cut in, &
Billy Payne's father, who couldn't find a job,
knocked out Billy's mother's eye, & my Uncle Jack
ran over a cliff in a lorry, & my dad who'd almost drowned
in burning oil more than once, & had lived a time in
a big place for people who couldn't remember, began to hate
my gran for something & so we left the north for his hometown
but he couldn't find a job & cursed those who'd stayed behind
& taken all the plums and not fought while he pumped petrol,
repaired radios, grew mushrooms, delivered milk, until
finally getting a job at the Ministry of Works all the while
fixing me with steel gray-green eyes, a bit of cinder in one
I couldn't take my eyes off, calling me all sorts of names.
Flash fast forward. After the funeral, one of his sisters
said to me, "I bet you're glad he's gone."
I didn't know that anybody knew.

THE THIRD FACE

"buggered by the father"
    —A. R. Ammons

1

I cry till I get my Scottish dancing pumps,
    soft as something I don't even know yet.
I wear them all the time. They are softer
    and more supple than skin. *Cissy.*
In my red hat I fold round myself.
    I endure the rot of school, debris
flying from all directions. Everybody
    talks. I am trying to listen.

2

It was all for the best. He meant well.
    [I bet you're glad he's gone.] He went,
but at the last moment a nurse's skirt
    almost changed his mind.
                                    A drunk
is starting to weep. I am in a role now,
    something like a friend, dreaming
a dream before there were fathers where
    I am in charge. I might be a character
in a story, someone making me up.
    But it's not open-ended.
There is denouement.

3

All mouths are merciless, kisses
acid. I look forward to the day when,
    all identity gone I call my inventions just
a child's cry, a walk in the dark.
    It doesn't work. His great hands still grip me.

He still calls me *Cunt. Cissy. Crippen.*
Everyone except him has at least two faces.
One of mine is a murderer's.
The other is hidden.
There's a third that's a vulture's.

WATCH YOURSELF

My father was polite, always insisting, for instance,
    that women climb ahead of him up the ladder
to the flat garage roof to see his prize tomatoes,
    or always insisting they sit in his new recliner
where they were too polite to protest as it tipped
    back, raising legs and thighs. Even on his deathbed
it was on his mind. I could see it in the way he watched
    the young Pakistani doctor, as if she were already
a sloe-eyed houri he'd half considered converting for—
not that he was religious, though he was convinced
there was life on other planets, and we had visitors.
    Tubes in arm and nose, he said if ever I wrote
a novel to make it full of sex: "sex sells." Hank Jansen
    was his favorite, with Lawrence and Henry Miller
close behind, though only read in parts. Propped
    by pillows, he who spoke little couldn't stop
talking about it, as if *it* could prevent the inevitable.
    There was the widow across the street, always
burning leaves, a sister in Canada, another dead,
    women in foreign ports, at work; the rich foreign
girls from local language schools mother took in
    to pay the bills after relatives he'd courted and
counted on died and left him nothing and the machine
    he invented to sharpen razor blades was ready
just at the time disposables hit the market. As he talked,
    I remembered mother saying how those girls cried
and carried on because she'd treated them so well
    and they couldn't bear to leave her. And on he went
with weekly trips to London, dressed to kill, "to see
    the paintings at the Tate." In great gilt frames,
his copies of Monet and Manet hung in living-room
    and dining-room, and everywhere else the walls
would bear them. "Olympia" and "Le Déjeuner sur l'Herbe"
    hung outside the bathroom door which had a hole
drilled into a corner panel, blocked with a matchstick stub
    when not in use. "So," he took a breath, "What do you
think of me now? More or less?" I lied, and left.
    He'd painted in the hot cramped airless attic, climbing up

and pulling the ladder after on an elaborate system of ropes
   and pulleys. After he died, I figured how it worked,
climbed up, crawled in. Stooping, I groped along the wall
   and found a switch. A naked woman loomed out of the dark.
I slipped on photographs and hit my head.
   The face was just sketched in, still incomplete, though
the body gleamed like marble. Breasts came at you, but
   the bushy arrow pointing down drew in your eyes, and then,
strangely, turned them round and made you watch yourself.

MY AUNT

"A new world is only a new mind."
—William Carlos Williams

I have decided to be happy and anonymous
    in a new world where even my father's
hateful face is that of a god's. Here
    strangers come together like rain
and beds are full of wisecracks. Now
    even automata become zanily unpredictable.
I can reinvent the usual, even improvise trees,
    and when alarms cry nothing happens.
Everybody knows there are no wolves.
    When I am done all this will be a flowerbed,
permanently surprised, intuitive and lovely
    with no memories. If there is any remembering
to be done it will be done by my aunt who cut him
    when he came at me for daring to look him in the face.
It was she, normally a timid woman, who took off
    her clothes and embarrassed everyone
by slinging them out the window—What I'll do to you
    if you don't leave the boy alone—where they fell into
February 1950 which is in my mind still on the cover
    of National Geographic. Who was I? I was ten.
That's me on the cover too, a look of surprise on my face,
    naked and black, while a stranger snaps me off
at the waist and all round breasts hang for everyone
    to point and giggle at in a civilized society
beyond the seas where they have seasons
    and play games so hard it hurts, where they eat children
for breakfast, and snacks. But I am not big enough yet
    to climb out of the picture. And where would I go?
I am happy here. I leave all that to my aunt, who is
    already taking off what little she has on, about to
hurl it at the camera and climb in after to sort things out again.

FENS

The old world of blues and grays and greens
   is now the black made by Dutchmen
who drained and dredged till soil shone
   like anthracite, shrinking year by year, giving up
coin or torque, bones and bog oaks that crack open
   like geodes, all mineral veins and ferns, forests brought
down by storms from the Urals, nothing to stop them until
   shoulder-high islands, Danea, Manea, Ely, Quy . . .
Here they held out, fenmen dark as Iberians,
   who walked on stilts, drawing in Roman or Saxon
or Norman to drown beneath peat-colored water,
   their dark eyes and skin still there in my wiry schoolmates,
the sons of farmers and laborers, and my grandfather whose
   Claud's six-feet driving wheels hauled "The Fenman,"
who drove the royal train to Sandringham, and who died
   before my birth but not before his hardness drove my father off
at fourteen to join the Navy and stay there thirty years,
   just as *he* then drove me off to where I now sit
among mountains in another land looking out at driving northeast rain,
   remembering a boy with a book, *Hereward the Wake,* who looks up
sharply at a bittern's boom in the reeds, already making up
   other lost places, silent as water, as the wind
before it gathers and heads on in.

DIS PATER

(i)

Heat tinkling like
  a keyboard, pyre for
consciousness until some
  last flame erupts in
a duststorm and I turn
  my back as the cat springs
to the tabletop and the voices
  of my children fade, thrashing
about in the distance as if
  their lives depended on it,

(ii)

while hunger on enormous wings
  remains, its flight thwarted
by squares of glass. I even own
  its echo that casts a shadow
more real than what it falls on.

(iii)

  Against my house and
down the back its vines throttle.
  It seems there is something
in the sky I can reach and cut
  free if I go upstairs, but
the stairs are loose. The world
  drops, even as the camera
paralyses, borrows and pays back
  just enough for me to drown in.

(iv)

When he died decades ago,
  my father loosened himself, but he
still hangs overhead, with

barrage balloons I remembered
like gray whales before I'd even
   seen a whale, waiting for one to burst
with ack-ack fire or V-2.

   (v)

   Damnation isn't just a saying,
a falling down a fissure. There's
   the mind. And he really was damned.
Damned in the life and in the dying
   to destroy whatever he touched.
Everything was meat for him,
   his equipment hosing down the sky,
snaking after anything, male or female,
   everything meat for his mouth.
"I thought it was cigars," hurling
   my first book, beautifully boxed
and inscribed to him, across the floor.

   (vi)

   I crawl from sleep to sleep, watching
the merest flick for food. In the thick
   of things nothing sets me apart.
I am hauled back night to night, waiting
   to be sprung on, waiting to spring,
grab everything and toss it beyond,
   make objects work for me,
their useless claws in the useless brain.

THE CODE

On sweaty nights the lilac fell back
    like a broken outboard motor, kicking off
dust. Day was an afterthought, folds
    of silk over the clatter of postures.
Plugging the background was a lake
    the air came out of, brightening as it
closed in, smelling of woodshavings
    and pelts, mindless as the drone
that comes from the bloodstream in
    extreme silence, the hum of nerves.
When done, the heat moved back
    to the edge and dripped over. I had
just been to see my father. From inside
    the flames he saw me and switched on
the TV, clicking channels until he
    found cartoons. A car drove off
behind him, and I found I meant
    the opposite of what I said. I said nothing.
I had a code where each prayer was
    a curse, each thought a scream,
and nothing was symbolic.

QUASAR

I catch a glimpse of me
  in the bathroom mirror, & it's
not me. My father looks out as he has, really,
  each day of my life. He leers, sticks out his tongue,
something pours from his mouth.
    He doesn't say anything. Doesn't have to.
If you went to his grave now you'd see it heaving
    like a fat laughing belly. I am falling
into his mouth. He pats me like a dog.
    No part of my body he doesn't know
as I lie on my back, pink belly exposed,
      tail wagging, squirming. And he orders me
to do unspeakable things, unspeakable,
      in the literal sense: you cannot speak them,
so no one will ever know. Then he tips me over
      with his foot & suddenly that's you staring out
the mirror, but there's no one to stare at.
      The room is empty, cold and white.
You were there a minute ago & now it's too late.
        You turn away, deeper into the glass
that stretches like quicksilver as far as you can see,
        sucking in everything from the outside world,
reflecting itself reflecting itself so you are in two or more places at once
          at least always & nothing can hold you back from tipping
over the edge except there is no edge unless the light in the glass should
                                                                    put
          itself out leaving like an unsteady quasar
scattering signals into deep space whose loneliness is a perfect match
          & mirror if ever it can find it.

OUTLINE

Winter has left its angels
  crusted with salt. The late March wind
grows in silence where remnants
  of sky roll toward one another.
I think of my father.
  He says he fought the Nazis
into the air, lured them
  into clouds, then begins to
gnaw another hole in the
  hospital blanket.
                  Currents
still flowing in dead flowers
  are his breath. The voices of smoke
and shrapnel are still in pursuit
  as I go check on her. There
she is in her chair, writing more
  proverbs into her huge book
where each proverb somehow
  cancels another out. You're
not half the man your father was,
  she says.
              Out the back door
I watch large drops hit early
  swallowtails, sending shudders
through their whole bodies,
  knocking them out of the air.

BIRDNESTING

I

The crow's black wings blat, to outlast
  bleakness, find sustenance there, while
I walk out again into anonymous snow
  thinking of names, foot in my foot,

in the deepest drifts I can remember,
  in steps that each time sink further
where there's no bottom. I am not yet
  used to people gone. There is no wind,

as if someone's holding it back. Not
  a needle moves.

II

           In my room
the only movement is my reflection in
  the window that passes through everything,

or everything passes through it. So it's not
  exactly nothing; here's everything I need.
But hooks are blunted, lines and flows
  frozen, everything inside and out reverted

to opposites in black and white. The eyes hurt,
  looking for a story, or at least a plot
other than the one I've grown used to where,
  having finally buried my father, I'm waiting

for my mother's death in another country.
  She's propped on a pillow, packed in linen,
fragile and complaining. Lonely, she rejects
  company. Hungry, she rejects food.

If I returned there, I'd take an axe
  and chop the house down, everything
in it.

   III

    A rooster from the lopsided
    house across the valley reaches into

my ears, stirring the memory of a kid
  sticking a pin into the ends of eggs,
blowing out generations of songbirds,
    linnet and thrush, chaffinch and yellowhammer,

saving the hollowed shells to hoard,
  as if beauty could live private,
as if what I loved could contain nothing.

THE POINT

My mother kneels at a pool
giving off its own life like a fantastic book.
As evening comes down, she sees me in the dark
at the margin looking for that one lost touch,
   a kind of paraphrase of touch, and a message,
even fragment, that would open my hand,
   even though I'm afraid of this primal vote
of life and limb, a stranger to the bridge.
   We were not a close family,
scarce family at all, so nothing could go wrong,
   but to make sure I left almost for ever.
I made my world clean as a seabird
   in the wind. But there she is connected
to herself in the pool, remembering
   in endlessness a concentrated someone who
went backwards to be more accessible
   to herself, and she turns and points at the real thing
which is not like the real thing at all,
   and starts to speak, but before she can finish
everything becomes extra and what had been
   like photography becomes a frame marked
Empty, and drowned faces flash like fish
   while I rustle and become a room to my own applause
dancing a Mr. Bones waving the leg of a calf.
   As light tilts, the whole sea sloshes over
and in the middle there she is still, my mother,
   kneeling at a pool, scrying, reciting in a foreign language
I can't even hear, but I think she's saying
   Let's work together. It was then I knew she wasn't
my mother. Old men don't have mothers.
   What would be the point?

HABEAS CORPUS

Knots, a thousand lights, in
   sheer dark, aimed at my window,
tinny crystals, so mother dies
   in my sleep. The snow turns
coarse, goes out. An axe sounds
   where I'd never heard an axe before.
Breathing becomes dangerous. I can't
   help it, making me her, even
before I was born, her brain burning
   out patterns I follow like will
o' the wisps, sparks popping.
   I put on heels and find I can balance,
twist my spine, bend to get my seams
   straight on my own, no one to
call on, like she called me, sheer nylon
   turning on sheer skin under my palms.
I pull on the ratty musquash coat.
   I have the body. I move off in it,
eddying, trying to see who I am now.
   I totter down the street thinking,
one day he'll be sorry. And here I am.
   Sorry. I watch her getting smaller
up the road. I watch us both, till
   nothing's all there is.

DEEP FISH

White sky like curtains
in a headlong dive onto
fields & farms. I look out
from windows cut down to size
where a broken wheel is
grinding over glass alongside
a whiplash of streams,
where whirlpools twist
leaves & detritus in
on themselves, like ecstasies
unmoored or abandonments
without consequences & in the room
behind me I can still pick up
rustlings in the pianola,
the canary I freed picking
to pieces wax flowers in the
parlor & the pedal-organ
playing hymns by itself beside
the conservatory & its tomatoes
forced by bull-blood, thinking
me thinking them, & in my pockets
pebbles & stones, plans for gravity,
& air raid shelters eaten by evening
& a voice like my mother's
coming at me, deep fish swimming up
from night to drown
in white sky

DARK SIDE OF THE MOON

Uncle Syd, Syd Barrett, Syd "The Beat" Barrett, whose name they took
  from his Anchor days playing bass with the Riverside Jazz Club,
and gave to the violet-eyed, violet-haired boy in the corner
  born Roger Keith. My father's cousin and best friend,
that's his god-father gift on my desk, a silver egg-cup, napkin ring,
  spoon, all with my initials, the date, and a card wishing me
"safe passage through these troubled times and a safe voyage through life."
  By day he was a clerk in David's Second-hand Bookstore
near the market, razoring the plates from rare books and
  selling them on the side. Most weeknights were The Stirlingaires,
his own dance band for weddings and such, cousin Tony
  on trombone. Weekends were the Anchor, above
the mill race. He had eyelids that hid what he was looking at.
  He made his own wines, elderberry, parsnip, potato, and
would offer me some, especially if I'd brought a girl with me.
  Here, he'd say. *Try this, and try my new chair. Push. See,
it reclines.* I always forgot to warn, and before she could prevent it,
  she was on her back, his eyes up her skirt. When he came up
our garden path—*Quick,* said my father. *Get upstairs!* Mother
  scuttled out of sight. And he too is long gone, but his name
goes on in this Syd who lives with his Mum in St. Margaret's Square,
  next door to my sister, who complains of the girls ("mostly Swiss")
who clamber over his fence and beat on his door, or push through
  her skimpy hedge and beat on *her* door calling his name.
They cry and sing, disbelieving her protests, until she has to call the police.
  But he's mostly quiet or invisible, though in summer he tends
his bonfires out back in khaki or bermuda shorts. "They say
  he burns his paintings," my sister says, "but I've never seen that.
What I do see sometimes is him in Sainsbury's or Marks,
  his cart piled high with Kotex and Maxipads and such. That's
what he does with his millions. I always know where he's been
  because a few days later the fire brigade pulls up and they all
hop off and knock politely on the door he's painted another color.
  A neighbor's called because of the stink, the drains. He sticks them
down the toilet blocking everything up." "Yes," I say, "blocked."
  "You know," she says, "you went to the County school with them lot.
Our cousins or something." "I don't know." "You know Waters. He's a
  foxhunting toff now. And Gilmour. That's Uncle Ted the butcher's

daughter's son. He looks a bit like you." "I don't know them," I say.
The sixties passed me by. Seventies too. "You don't know anything.
How long is it since you paid us a visit? Where have you been?
Hardly a postcard. You're from another planet."
It was true. Somewhere on the dark side. Out of touch.

TEMPORAL

A speck of gray fire reveals
a flickering cheap room, my coat
on the bed, and a water-glass.
They float like flowers on a pond
tossed by someone who just left.
The silence is like someone reading
Braille. Did I think nothing
would change? This is the nightmare
I've walked into and it opens for me.
Something's dying. There is a muttering
though nothing much has happened yet.
It is still a bright day outside.
There is something in it like other days
though now cars are driving around
with their headlights on. This is
my story, but there's a limit to what
I can say, and the time to say it.
I hold up my face in front of me, and
lay it down. It blows away, vapid
as a mud flat. It cries out for someone
to take a hammer to it and yell Liar, Fake.
At the center of the room is a sound
like singing, but is not singing.
It falters, and quits. It is my mouth.
And a pattern emerges the way
a grass falls down a blade.

THE PSYCHOANALYSIS OF FIRE

I'm thinking of how I'd grabbed
the glowing coal but wouldn't
open my child's fist
grasping it tighter the more
it burned till my mother pried
each finger free, as I watch
a lively bed flicked by flames that dart
about the top like Ariel
while others work steadfast
at one spot, working it
through, working through
it to bright bells, carillon
of changes, & the log's
black skin squares off, flaking
under softer flames heavy with
the unburned, flaring up &
over again & again toward
the stove-pipe that sucks them up
while bolts of new blue silk drift over
the crumbling body of the log,
& that's how I'll be, leaving,
totally absorbed, but not just
yet as flesh that will never crumble
floats into my mind, bodies so
smooth they're air, breasts
that need never fear the x-ray,
& sailing up the coast
catching the scent of sweet
medicine grass, perfumes of pine
& flowers like the New World
of which sailors said "the land
is smelled before it's seen,"
& once ashore approaching a basket
on the beach, a conch, a thatched hut
& a small head poking out,
bellies rounded like the snow outside
on the windy deck at night on which
the fire reflects, dying silently, separate

yet intimate, the water hissing
& heaving on the black stove
like the pleasure of an impossible longing.

RAIN OF THE WALDENSIANS

Late rain, humble, dedicated to the quiet virtues.
Rain falling on the Anatolian Bird Goddess
I bought in Turkey and placed in the arbor,
falling on the painting of St. Kevin I bought in Dublin
and placed on the porch, where he hatches
a nest of blackbirds in his hands.

From wood and hill the rain echoes like the bell
in which Modomnoc carried bees across the pure-colored sea
in a small boat sailing from the east. This rain
in plain dress cherishes the hidden seed: earnest and
humble craftsfolk about to stir their pale shoulders,
transform themselves and all around, turn inside-out
to form the coming reformation.

Objects all around me are silent and alone. Silence
is their speech and mine. From the blackness rain's
attracted to my light, its songs adagio, andante, crescendo,
diminuendo to the voices of things extinct. It runs along
whole fronts, wide curtains, whole centuries. It rains
my Huguenot great-great-grandmother from Cevennes,
part of Pope Clement's "execrable race of the ancient Albigensians."
It rains those weavers, their caged birds and window boxes,
Friendly Societies and flower shows.

Next morning, an old lady watches drops slip off the ends
of mulberry leaves onto beans rising from underwater
to send out tendrils. Some she sees find nothing to grasp
and curl in on themselves. Some touch string, stick, and climb.
Others ascend themselves, or in mutual aid bridge synapses
one over another. The whole group is a nerve until they flower,
and then she'll say, "now they can breath." She calls the cat.
He comes home late, splashing along the streambed like a small boy.

CONSUMED

"In girum imus nocte et consumimur igni"
   —*Latin palindrome*

                  like a tourist
W ho cannot leave while the town &
E nvirons are still lit up beyond midnight & multi-
C olored bunting hangs out as if
I t is always like that, I keep circling, avid phantom
R eady for anything, holding on tight, seldom
C learing things by more than a few inches—the trick's not to
L ook down or slow up, keep faking fast, changing
E xpressions to respond to everything even before
I t happens, totally prepared, as if I believed we could all
N ow have something in common & can respond to that feeling,
T elling myself at any moment life is sure to take over, as I'd
H oped it always would, whisk us all away to live in one garden not
E ven a few beats away on angel-wing where
N ot a flower that flares & falters
I s lost when the angel of night appears
G athering hot pearls to hang on her black skin, then
H olding back skirts to reveal a child gripping live coals
T ight, coals under his tongue, staring at you.
A nd you know him, know he can't let go, can't let them drop. So
N ow you take his hand. Together you walk
D own the narrow path where flames lick, and we
A re slowly consumed by fire,
                  like a tourist

ARS AMATORIA

DE PROFUNDIS

"Out of the deep, child, out of the deep"

The deck just gave way. At first you could
hear nothing. Then the gunwale caved in, then
      the hull groaned & cracked. Pretty soon fingers
were clutching at anything, but it was all
      slippery as fish. Then the switchboard
lit up in a number of directions, mindless
          as headlights reaching into night,
trying to predict when the next world would loom up,
grasp at you, crash down, give way, but it kept
snagging birds, catching blossoms bright as chandeliers,
      masking pure weight as a momentary pause
while you tripped over yourself trying
      to make things do what they didn't
want to so nothing knew where or what
      it was, & you couldn't see yourself
      because mirrors were still misty & fragments
so you tried not to make too much noise among the
      twisting breakers & you sought the
rumbles of shoals glancing off the nonlight
      on the other side
      forcing you to breathe a little longer
before being swamped & forced deeper till
      up you bobbed to the surface,
tumbling & dipping like a melting ice-floe,
naked innocent & dumb

CALENDAR GIRL

The nymph sits in her cave, naked.
The deckchair lusts after the strange trees.
She cups her chin: *I love you.*
Each evening I return to her though
the divorcee next door who sunbathes on her lawn
has a big chest with a few
black hairs. When I take the nymph to school
& unroll her she says: *I love him.*
She's keen on sports. Me too. When I get home
I forget I'm tired, but tired I am.
She has that effect. I crawl along my branch
like a chameleon, watching her with my
swivel eyes. My tongue is sticky.
She understands. I watch her try to move.
She twitches. Suddenly she's
outside the window. My fingers open.
Something is undone before it's done.
The divorcee. I stand up so fast I knock
the binoculars off the National Geographics
& onto the floor. Freeze. *Turn on the radio.*
It shouts something about cold light & old men.
She smelled of skin. I know how to swim.
Voulezvous swimmez avec moi? Ah,
she's left her face in the mirror.
I lick it. She would understand. Now
watch me ride onto your lawns, destroy
your cities, rape your women till they
glint like large diamonds. It starts to rain.
Smell of beans downstairs on the stove.
I look out. She has me
where she wants me.

GONADS

"Any questions?" asked the evangelical physician lecturing
on Sex-and-Marriage to a roomful of young born-again Crusaders
who, if we'd been allowed to squirm would have long-since squirmed
right out of our short gray pants, ties and striped blazers.
But we sat silent in the warm room, avoiding eyes, till fatty
in the front broke and blurted: "Sir, er, um—what is the chemical
constituency of mother's milk?" Next day, in Biology, I was banished
to the back among the masturbators where I tried to figure out
how I'd been such a fool as to ask what gonads were. I really
didn't know, but there it was written on the board at the end
of a long arrow stuck into a groin: Gonads. I also used my time
at the rear to practice the correct pronunciation of "vagina," a word,
until that weekend, I'd only mouthed quietly to myself from
my father's plain-wrapped book found at the bottom of his carved
mahogany chest. As the word blossomed from page to page
I'd whispered it the Latin way, "wagina," first declension feminine,
nominative case, long "ee," "eena." Now I repeated to myself,
quietly, I thought, "vagina, vagina, vagina." I ended up
outside the headmaster's office, and as I waited recalled a story
in the book of boys being made eunuchs for harems by being bounced
up and down on a horse's spine. When the door opened, I had moved on
to "carezza," a way of riding pillion, the naked girl's hair streaming
back across the naked young man's face. After school, no one home,
I consoled myself for still-smarting buttocks by digging out the book
and following "vagina" up and down pages like fresh tracks to somewhere,
I wasn't sure where, but fragrant and exciting. Like the day later
that summer when I decided to follow the advantage of an empty house
and climb through the trapdoor in the ceiling I'd often wondered about.
It was above the heavy chest, outside the bathroom door. I'd drop in
on Mrs. Petrie, our neighbor, a divorcee with a son my age,
a boarding-school twit only home on holidays. She was out all day,
but sometimes on weekends I saw her over the garden wall, sunbathing.
I'd go through her drawers, look in her wardrobe, rifle through
linen closets. Heart in my ears, I stood on the box, pushed open
the hatch, did a hard chin-up, scrambled to a seat, legs dangling.
I looked around the musky dark, left to where one end of the terraced
houses

must be, right to the other. I could drop in on anyone, discover anything
I wanted, and nobody would ever be the wiser—better than "Murders
in the Rue Morgue"! So I carefully pulled up my legs and stood on
the beam. I slid a foot forward onto what seemed solid. The crash echoed
up and down the attics, one end of the street to the other.
I just had time to look down through the dust of plaster and lathe
and see a foot dangling over nothing before the floor gave way again
on the other side and I landed on my gonads. I rode the beam and the
pain
that was only slightly muted by the panic that set in when I realized
the problems I'd have explaining *this*, if ever I got down.

THE WIND AND THE RAIN

You wonder if you'd recognize them now,
   the girls in elementary school, Glynnis,
for example, tall with glasses, who
   brought in a cardboard sheet and bicycle lamp
to demonstrate the after-image, the mind
   fooling itself, seeing what is no longer
there; or Christine who brought the local Icini
   queen to life, Boudicca of the flaming hair
and scything Raleigh wheels. She
   could outrun and outjump all us boys,
which later helped me understand how
   Atalanta could beat out Melanion,
and why he had to cheat.
   And then the gorgeous Rhoda, all of ten,
who crawled around the classroom floor,
   pretending to pick up the stuff
she'd dropped, but really looking up
   the boys' gray shorts to taunt us
in the recess. All were afraid of her,
   and some in love. "I know what the doctor did,"
she sang when Dr. Broda (recently joined
   in holy matrimony with Dr. Fuchs, the
famous atom spy) had cupped our small
   embarrassed balls and ordered us to cough.
Later, Rhoda's father, Brin, a Welshman
   quick on the birch, was my Headmaster at
the Cambs High School for Boys. In church,
   he sat behind me in the choir, keeping us
boy sopranos all in line, enemy of whispers,
   Malvolio to our gum and fidgets. And then,
one day, father, mother, brother, Rhoda,
   all left for Australia, and that was that.
Until, years later, when I too had left
   the sinking ship, I opened up a paper to
Profumo's trial. "Please state your name,"
   the judge intoned. "Rhoda Newton-John."
"And state your occupation." "Whore, m'lud."
   And that was that. More years go by. I turn

on the TV. And there she is, years shed
   like skin, but sweeter, blander, singing
some soft song, all changed, her name
   changed too: Olivia.

When that I was but a little tiny boy,
   With hey, ho, the wind and the rain;
A foolish thing was but a toy,
   For the rain it raineth every day.

TURN OF THE YEARS

I scrub the floor of our new house, she polishes the sink.
   Both pick up flies. When we drink well-water, air fattens
and day begins along its widening channel, slowing the wildness
   of bobcat & coyote, shaping trees with a fuller silence.
The sun sticks in windows as if it had always grown there.
   Our images too freeze in them, middle-aged, then
tear free & go spilling about like gallons of light.
   Come night, as blood's tide pulls back
we fly. This house is nothing like those where each of us was born.
   And then it is first winter, our parallel tracks
doing parallel things. Hers stop at a message in snow
   neither of us scratched. Mine follow suit. Then—
flash. We watch blossoms barely touch the twigs
   & go. Flash. Warp of August, & a wind cutting across the
telephone wire tells yet another story we'd never heard before.
   Hot, hot. We sit in brightness, trying to sort out sequences
as light becomes deer increasing to hold their own against winter
   already here along the stone wall where the branches
of our old leafless maples loom up against the changing horizon,
   pulse on/off, filaments inside a bulb, as the sun hits
around clouds in a surge & hides in release, systole,
   diastole. Some crazy creature over them is dancing as certain
of winter as it was certain of summer, its voices finding
   a route for mountains clearer now we have grown into them.
The goddess palms her eggs like stones & slips them
   under graying moss & bark, far into the music we can hear now,
where the unborn get ready to hunker down again.
                                                      If soul can sing
it must break; gamble its wings for a clown suit,
   find songs that fix crooked doors, put up storm windows,
take down screens, wash the floors, clean the windows, stretching
   from the inside for the high deep stains, collect the flies.

THE RAIN

                    gliding in slowly, at a
human height, then swooping up
grazing the Homestead before falling
back to meet me here
in the other life of newt & worm,
stream & seizure, sometimes
barely holding it together
when something in the rain slips
past into the mind & it responds
with events before they've happened,
then reversing into panic,
continuing backwards into
knee-high hills where it shoots
into forward & goes crashing
through the windshield laughing
at a child accumulating itself
only to turn into a life of
furnished rooms & gas-fires,
foreign cities, losses, age.
But one day something stands up
out of the storm & I can trace
her shape & follow her as though
she was an old friend before
she split like a echo. Now,
after the rains, in the rich
loamy scent of a female world,
one I'd known as a child,
I listen again for what might be
hidden on the other side,
like silence carved from noise,
or the richness inside rock.

ARS AMATORIA: CHORUS FOR ST. VALENTINE'S DAY

STROPHE

Bird tracks I followed from feeder across snow,
  across snow from feeder bird tracks
that disappeared into chiasmus then reappeared
  from under the book I'd left open as I fell asleep
& hopped into my mind dreaming of time as
  an enormous light inside a bear in his cave
seeming to die, but no, the glamour is still on him,
  while the great sickle rises over him
in a billion billion volts & night wears on
  & great distance & time stops here
where my wife is asleep & naked beside me

ANTISTROPHE

In the morning I find myself standing
where the bobcat bit a meadow vole in half,
  her hind legs sticking out of the snow & not a speck
of blood, as if she is coming out of a bloodless dream
  backwards or diving headfirst for figurines
in some wintry wreck. Am I too old for saints?

STROPHE

I am standing again in night up to my waist,
wanting to shout *encore* to the whole scene
  & mean it, my gray whiskers flaring behind
the woods, silver wire pointing to dwarf stars,
  bloody lips chomping on the white arm beside me,
on the stumps of unreason swollen the way pebbles
  light up underwater to make unthought-of dark flowers

ANTISTROPHE

The lady lies on clean sheets, eyes scanning the black sea,
    until beside her a seal's face breaks the surface,
opens his mouth, tries to chew sky & spit stars
    like words & music, but what comes out are little birds
making a living, making do, making tracks across the blank page
    of an implausible sky, tracks she follows

RIDDLE: CONTRA MORTEM

"see how it is velvety how its innerness clings"
—*Hayden Carruth, "Contra Mortem"*

Flowers, let's say. Yes, flowers—petals, perfume; flowers
lavish, lotus, cyclamen, rose, or more austere, daisy, marigold, ling.
But tides too, lapsing and rising, reaching and falling back,
leaving rockledges and limpets, oranges, gull feathers, small fish,
the smell of small fish and algae. A wheel, or that nothing
at the core that makes the wheel. Oh, just about everything—
lilac, its voice, the bog that cradled Tolland man, the source
in the mountains, caves there with painted walls, wisent,
auroch, elk, the ochre handprints, some missing finger-joints,
gaping salmon carved from an antler, scored. It's where the earth
goes in winter, the holy hallway. Fish, addled, climb its ladder in spring.
It's a mirage, a house—the heart breaks here. Metaphors mass at its

gates—

It is perpetual allusiveness. It is Pegasus riding itself to melodies
by Grieg and Debussy, dissonance by Satie. It has always been here
since the birth of Venus. It is the mouth of the megalopolis.
It is her walking down the stairs in a very short skirt.

YOGA

She who has never followed instructions has followed them now
    for some time as if her life depended on it.
She twists herself into such positions it's hard to recognize her
    as she's cobra or lion, rabbit or dog, crocodile, locust,
or subtle pigeon, her favorite. There she is now, her long
    swan neck over her shoulder, *rere regardant,* or
regarding nothing, a "concentrated expression of being."
    Intertwined with herself she's in opposite places at once,
space measured and refined. Brother Ass is now caduceus,
    Möbius strip, parts interchanged. *Me and my shadows,*
she's said. She gathers them up, repeating patterns,
    changing to pure form, supple as fish, a fugue
of variations. And sometimes, in the whorls and twists,
    the stretches that seem to end where they could go on
and on, in some place unrecognizable to me but
    discovery for her, there, I think, is when she finally starts
to meet herself, the contours and details of her life
    concentrated into a mountain pose secure and restrained
yet free, from which she comes back down as if
    she had never been anywhere. But she has.

MORE

I watch her leave, go down, around: lost.
Pick her out later where the road's
a line, could be a sunken wall. She moves
against the snow that coats the mountainside,
past appletrees she emptied some weeks back,
chugging slowly upward, becoming cedar as
she's lost in it, emerging blacker, a sharper speck,
becoming briefly the stone wall that drives straight up,
walking over the roof of a barn in disrepair,
past a white house that almost isn't there,
then the slow climb south until she's lost
in broken landscape where she is & isn't
till she isn't & I have to follow blind
where she will turn downhill, past the farm
for sale, a needle backing round to north,
along the red kill & the dairy farm for sale,
to reappear through woods, treading in
her old steps, growing from speck to spinnaker
as she billows up the just-ploughed drive,
gathering everything back in, bringing it
inside with her, so when I lift my eyes
back where she's been it's all there still,
in place, but somewhere else, and more.

MORNING

I scrape at my face in the dark
and look back to the bedroom
where she sleeps on her side,
legs to chest, as she has slept all our life together.
She goes somewhere, and is still there.
I scrape over my scar that slides from mouth
to ear as if something had been let out.
It is not yet dawn. I have to wait to
go out to do what I've done for decades,
though as the young get younger
I have less to teach them. I try to question
what I believe, as if I really believed it.
But I'll let it slide, say the same things.
I turn back and watch her.
When she wakes I won't be here,
but her face, younger now than when we met,
will wake, as if night gave her something
it had always intended to take away.
It will always be a face from before we met,
before knives, before sickness, even from
before words. This evening she will tell me
she dreamed about eternal life. For now, however,
I stand, face raw, watching not where she is,
not her, but somewhere else and someone
now part me, though alone where we must always
be alone, together everywhere else,
our lives right in our faces.

SHADOWS AND DISTANCE

"What did I plan to say to her . . ."
—William Carlos Williams, *"Waiting"*

(i)

The gate thuds. My tongue is braced.
   Returning from town, voices are split
and spill all over.
                I split out the back
   where cold air tightens
to a mirror in which things seem
   too big.
             Here water is cunning
and hides everywhere, waiting. A
   windblown sheet could lurk
in a mote of dust and the sky
   knock itself to pieces.

(ii)

               From rockveins
shadows surge wave
   on wave. There's anarchy in
their contours but if there were
   none everything would be upside-
down. You'd find stars in your batter,
   planets in your bed. On whim,
everything could become the
   shortest day or longest night.
Breath would be optional and deserts
   wear you like shoes.

(iii)

              The wind's
dry as the peonies I gave her
   weeks ago. It has quenched itself
and sounds like children sleeping.
   I take a deep breath and go
back in.
          As someone once said,
   we only cross, the distance never changes.

THE STAR

You're writing down next spring's
   garden: beans, tomatoes, squash
& so on. Outside, snow sticks everywhere,
   clogging everything up, hemming

You in. When done you pick up
   the newspaper. In the obits
there's always someone you know.
   They come & go, & you never

Quite get used to it. Walking
   slowly downstairs you call
to your wife: How about a game
   of cards? OK. She shuffles, deals,

Lifts her head. Look, she says,
   That huge star. I've never seen
anything like it before. It looks like,
   who knows. You turn & see it,

Whiter than snow, insistent as stone.
   Imagine, she says, what a place
like that must be.
   And drops her hand.

THE WANDERER

Ðonne onwæcneð eft   wineleas guma

The swallow's shadow   has no use,
  but it angles in   for a moment
and moves on.
                 I smell the trees
but don't   recognize them.
Last night's still an image: I swam
  between the bars   into blueness but
the main sequence   was conflagration.
  Something made   space in the air
suffocating the birds.   Something
  got its wings stuck   and the sky
broke up.
             Over the city a wind
  whistles and whirls.   Newspapers
tumble over and over,   traveling
  backwards, in love   with their own
movements.
             In the evening things
  will come home again,   traveling
backwards, phrasing sorrow   as dignity.
  The periphery   used to have a
kind of serenity,   like a dried-up riverbed.
  Now it crumbles.
             I remember another
body, its expanse   and healing presences.
  How the   main road was filled
with women, naked   and lonely as beacons.

READING THE SIGNS

A voice under the half-moon.
  In late May it is not the sea
but the sound of the sea,
  a concave sound floundering
like memory. The sky
  is compressed, eroded to tinsel.
Something is taking place,
  a recurrence like samsara,
but nowhere and nothing
  is endless, I hope.
I try to escape in the car
  and a bottle. Move. Move.
The odor of musk is still on
  the front seat, along with various
violations of the moral order.
  Like Malvolio, I too was once
beloved. I drive on, pulling my voice
  in after, slipping from shadow
to shadow like a sneak. I wish
  it could be otherwise, so I try
to celebrate all wasted lives
  in song until I arrive at the edge
and get out. Footprints in the sand
  twist away from me. They may
be more than they seem. A single
  stream mutters, mediating loneliness.
I read the signs under a half-moon
  but have no idea what they mean.
I get in and drive back.

BASSO-RELIEVO

That feeling as a kid—double the limbs,
two of everything, rolled into a ball,
traveling in any direction. That sense
of omnipotence, unblemished by sex
(Aristophanes says people then propagated
like grasshoppers, shed seed in furrows.)
Until that sense of omnipotence challenged
the Father, and was cut down to size,
or cut straight down the middle, split
from that primeval state. The surgeon
was that Apollo of reason, moderation,
self-control. Split like a sorb-apple
for pickling. This was the way of humility.
But things did not go well. Loneliness
came into the world, recognition of self
and not-self. And when these halves
found other halves they'd clasp, and not
let go, even through starving, even though
they suffered from self-neglect.
So Zeus moved their sex up front;
some sort of stop-gap, pacifier. That
made things worse. So now we have
knowledge and yearning. And the threat
from on high that if we ever try to
reunite, we will be halved again.
But I am already basso-relievo on
this old tomb. All profile: one leg,
one arm, no back or front, no past or
present, staring ahead in stone.

SOMEONE ELSE'S SONG

I can still see her barefoot on the porch.
   Perhaps she is remembering the terrible
old couple who closed their eyes and groaned
   before the marriage could figure out itself
just when the mirror would fall and crack.
   She shivers as if in sleep. She is watching
a ghost of wind, nothing, until she turns
   and looks straight through me. Is she
thinking the same as this poem? Does what
   it think affect her? She sits in the shade
despite not because of the sun, but
   there is only me on the porch watching
random counterbalancings at the edge of
   something. The baby's slept all day. I see
the train rolling over the trestle the way actions
   overwhelm intent. The crescent river gleams
as if it couldn't end. A gust shivers on the window
   and slips beneath. She thinks: God doesn't seem
to learn from his mistakes. Yet her life is now
   somehow sufficient as she looks down
and watches lodged boulders, wondering
   if the bridge can take the weight. Perhaps, like me,
she feels unprovable, focused on an image
   that will not wake, as if she's staring at
the cells that make her soul, milling like dust motes
   caught in the sun. And now the mountains
step out of the light, a shock that focuses
   to a kind of conclusion. The train picks up
speed and heads straight for them, and she
   stops worrying about going the wrong way
or me on the bare porch with the baby waking,
   evening breaking about us, each shard
someone singing someone else's song.

CATCH

"I have never been inspired by sex."
   —Kenneth Koch

They shine already, a labor to haul in,
   to catch their flames, great labor
in beauty, strange to us, grown compact
   swallowed up in this dark world, its
green margins, their eyes cloud, here's
   my mouth, fractured bones flung away,
these strangers sing like dust, balanced
   like shadows, now they are tense,
now lax where I cannot stay and if
   they cry I can't hear, they probably
have little to say except how blind
   the scrutiny in this heavier world,
its compulsions, its indifferent energies,
   its engines unfocused but with a thirst
to catch and destroy, nothing
   escapes, so I am leaving while I can,
I've tasted enough. I am not hungry.

DAUGHTER

In April dusk the derricks stand,
   unspent. Sawdust lingers on
dirty pools and lightning flicks
   everywhere in subtle shades of lilac
by which I watched her. She only stirred
   but did not wake. What can I do
for the child? I am bound to a river
   turning itself, still buzzing. There's nothing
in this house, just pine knots in floors that
   prop each other up. Between flashes,
I can see a woman under a lamp
   reflected on the street. It is
all too familiar, the freighters anchored
   and the skunks scavenging on the back steps.
Child of my dotage, child of my imagination,
   I will give you my bench to work on
and my house to have. I have tried in monologue
   to bring you into being, draw you
from my head and make you as different
   from me as possible, celebrate
the silence between us which makes us,
   so I can affirm you in your being
and you affirm me attendant in a story
   going back generations through women
I can't know except through you.
   Down here, I am the last of the mist-men,
believing I can hear you breathe, my mouth
   filled with dust, the flesh faltering, one long
slow stutter, one long stumble, voiceless
   as the sacks that sit waiting to be loaded,
where night's girder is a kind of accolade
   in that it has not yet some crashing down,
held up by the gentle breathing of
   an only daughter sleeping in the glow
of the unspoken, while her breath
   escapes out the window I opened
to let in the faint taint of lilac
   and the ghost of the sea.

SOMEWHERE

"We are occupied by gods. The mistake is to identify with the god occupying you."
    —Carl Jung

He takes the ivory swan he's been carving
    for weeks and gives it to his daughter. "What's this
for?" she says, laying it aside. Passing through
    a door smaller than himself, he walks in dust
where footsteps fade like fishes.
    His wife barely looks over from
flapping laundry held back by wooden pegs.
    A breeze shivers in the bushes. He shivers,
and stops. His bones get up and walk away,
    push on in weather now like a musty attic.
Light shines through him and he cannot stop it.
    He decides to follow to somewhere unpronounceable
where swans can swim back where they came from.

PAINTING BY ANON

Like stone unconsecrated, I lost
feeling. Clearly, every year
wills us dead. But at the end
of the transept I saw him dancing
as if he didn't have to, and felt
better. Then, like madness,
a coldness interwove again
its sad conjecture until from a
stained-glass tree a body
hung as if it wanted to, fingers
spilling birds and birds, and from
the head fauns and phalloi.
At his feet stiff milkweed sprayed
seeds across the water and behind,
toward the lights, a fish-line snaked out,
and behind that scrolls of nets
from trawlers drifting off.
This is the kind of thing you'd expect
from Etruscan tombs, where death
is life. At Veii, for example, where
I coupled alongside the rock-cut
water courses, the ritual bathing-places
in the woods, beside the tombs,
among the glitterings and purlings,
the jigging scraps of light scattering
like insects, coming back together,
like art contracting and expanding,
pulling together memories of the invented past.

THE ECONOMY OF WINDMILLS

These are just windmills, or images
   of windmills, for now they make nothing,
trading in tourists. We file them away.
   Seen. The sky is blue, the sails blat round
in it, disappearing into themselves.
   There's a power-station down the road
and fields of tulips cavort in a bland mania,
   tulpenwoerde. All's well. It's hard to imagine
Don Quixote tangling with these. At their feet
   a stream makes uncertain progress
over rocks; obstacles fix its pace. I look up:
   turmoil in quiet sky, high in the rack.
Clavileño couldn't fly there, where the main star
   sails on above the *whump whump whump,*
the whooshing and woolgathering making good time,
   pulling in air, stirring it until dark gets
sucked into the airy trade too, *windhandel,*
   and is bottomed out, dropping to nothing.
The wind has shared what it could, and
   has shifted away, speculating in currents
over the North Atlantic, stirring them
   like memories of desire, or great gain.

ESCHATOLOGY

EXIST

As a kid I never thought of "pain" as
    something I felt. What I felt I could not
name or share. Now out the window I watch
    a thin chemical yellow smear being
pushed down by gray rolls of night. Behind me
            the physics of the TV screen

Plays out plots and previews. Outside is shapes
    moving under neon like those who have
already moved on. Lighted windows stick
    in the sky, independent of stone or
brick. I can only exist in writing,
            when for a while I do not know

I "exist." I exist only when I
    don't exist? There I am at the window,
staring back at me, in glass, dependent
    on the dark. In a room beyond this one,
I see myself in replicas that come &
            go with light, most there when most dark.

ESCHATOLOGY

The small body discovers the body dies, but
If it were a blackbird it would come back
Year after year and not stay down.
It is aware the world has seams.

Later yearning in hard dark, she has
The hummingbird fly out of its epidermis
As a lover would to feel the leaving,
And from the peel another bird double back

Into a rainbow. It is lovely, the whole range.
Now it will be all right. The world will race
And glow again like rivers. Imagine: All it takes is,
"What shall I tell myself?" And you have

A photo of a place you've never been
That takes you there, rapt in calm and quiet,
Intense and aureate, part of an evolving
Conversation that includes chasms that close

When you look at them, like in a fairytale,
And open too, done and undone the same,
And what was sitting on your chest
To stop your breath is now a marvel

You can enter as if it were ordinary,
Somewhere in a future that does not punish
But continues in different weather,
Much the same as this.

LOST CONSTELLATIONS

I blow on the fire to help it find its wood.
The corners of the room are askew.
The flies have knuckles hard as teak.
They bang out sentences on the insides of lampshades,
as if it were a party game.
A skull sits on its occiput by the window,
looking up among glass fused by the fire of an old house.

As you get on, your nails take longer to grow.
Your nose gets wider, and longer. Your skull gets thicker.
The erection that at twenty was ten degrees from vertical,
and at thirty dipped to forty-five,
by forty barely manages to stick straight out.
At fifty it's way below and falling.
It calls for protractor and compass—this old sailor
that once sailed by the stars and wind and
"the sweet sassafras smoke that's driven out to sea,
so the land is smelled before it's seen."

Now the blood would still mount to Perseus, Cetus,
Pegasus, Equeus, as he faces directly out of autumn's galaxy.
Just Mars is left. All the other planets are lost
behind the sun's glare. But scents still drift down
from lost constellations. Waves of space break.
It's the River Jordan spreading across night sands . . .

ORDERLY

It drew in my eyes, a slab, on it a huge white fish
just landed, or beached, a beluga, intact, naked,
no escape, lights flat silver and relentless, half on,
humming, as in the cramped space I tried to walk
around it, my first day, just eighteen, and as it drew me
to it, forcing my head round between legs splayed
as if securely asleep, I tried to block out the face
that watched, long gray hair loose, lying softly
over shoulders and flat breasts, horror and indignity and shame,
then a click made me jump and the lights came on
all round full as in a theater after the curtain falls,
and he slouched in, high rubber boots turned over
at the top and a long yellow rubber apron squeaking
like Homer's ghosts, and as he hosed down the floor
bits of flesh jumped up and stuck to him, staying there
when he turned the water off, sat down on a stool,
opened a brown paper bag and took out a sandwich
carefully wrapped in wax paper, meat sticking out the sides,
and my eyes could not move from the flecks that
clung to him as he ate and swallowed without chewing
or looking up and I couldn't move out of the way of what
I saw as it came at me, as if this was the way of things.

THREE SCORE AND THEN SOME

Panicked, I split. He one way,
I another. I come upon him
huddled in the woods, an echo
repeating no sound, catching
his breath. I pull him to his feet.
Let's go, I say. Look on the
bright side. Miles to go. We
pick up branches and pile them
on each other. We laugh, making
rocks sway, take on shapes
like in the old days. A few more
turns round the field and the sun
shoots up head-high, squawking
and creaking. Everything's flashing,
so we go on, collecting, two birds
hell-bent with rain starting to form
other beings that dovetail ours
with incompletions and fragments
beginning to relax into themselves,
each drop a spark leavening itself
big enough for us to wander through
as if for ever. And there we go,
haunted by ourselves, clearing the air,
floating through windows, limber,
roots wide as ships, on roads that
wander over and through the air
about us, glossy, dethroned, joyful
in our own funeral, split like an atom,
unmapped, bright, companionable, and cold.

HIV

My brother, the choreographer, still moves like a dancer,
   as if he, lifted above the ravages, has a dozen scripts
in his mind at once demanding immediate expression as one.
   He has announced he could think of what he had done
with his life as a theme for a vicious youngster
   whose instinctive impulse was submission. But ever since
the freedom of boys became a no man's land, he is eager,
   gun to crumbling temple, to get the job done.
So all his references are to one another. It is the visitor
   who interprets, sees the final results: a serpentine
dance among spools and pulleys. The dance itself
   sets the machine in motion. The motion keeps the dance
afloat. Every time he puts it on, he is surprised
   at the results: he has become his own administrator.
He keeps in touch with himself by watching the audience
   as the dance becomes the reel thing that can unwind forever,
with himself now its figment, reflected in the onlookers.

WORDS

She sits, crossing and re-crossing her legs;
    red toenails glint. She has slept. She is quiet
on a raffia chair that has seen better days.
    The radio is set off the dial. I could see up her thighs
if I didn't keep drawing her shawl over them.
    Nothing is an earthly color, benches floating
in lingering mist, trees a faded fresco of pillars
    turning back ripples that furl in gathering heat.
She's waited for the artist's life, but exposed nothing,
    hiding it all so there was nothing to give back,
just a grief that doesn't know it's grief.
    And now she has countries at her feet,
sadness banished. Now she shares secrets,
    and that's how we spend these morning visits,
talking, while she pretends to smoke. *At night*
    I'm afraid of snakes. One bit me. She pulls the shawl
over her head. *I have a moustache, and they call me*
    Your Excellency. I have to keep my frog legs
under wraps. How comforting these ghosts in
    white coats. Will you put me in a poem?
Can we leave? She's a compendium, and you
    are not sure she isn't now the work she wanted to create.
She may keep her teeth under the bed, but she still
    speaks fluent Cree learned from books. "Nistese,"
she calls me, Older Brother, but I am just a bruise
    because I still see her naked, washing her long legs
in a mountain stream that comes down like a message
    from even clearer waters. I still see her quick
as a naiad whose skin is all movement, or a dryad,
    dappled. This is my sister through whom
I am trying to read a world before my face
    in letters I can scarce make out, words I can't say.

LE GRAND MAL

Startled by the gradual
  but guided by hands that
grab weeds from anywhere
  to steady as they come
to life all round her, when
  unnatural lights grow
longer with all details
  left out she has nothing
else to do but release
  her arms' spiral that looks
like flying but as they
  spin they efface themselves,
going underground in
  a fine frenzy, Dis-seized
to where sky's so hard
  it's all angles and there
by a low fire she finds
  the shadow selves that rock
in dark tides till she sees
  their spirits rise flat
as blue slate and counts them
  like hard breaths until she
adds up again, bobbing to the
  surface like a swamped
trunk, her head starting to talk
  as if ordinary and she hears
her body, at first like a puppet's
  jangling and then clear as
oxygen, as rain as it fills her
  cool shadow so she knows
she's joining up again, what
  to take and what to leave to hold
the brimming back that's always
  poised to overwhelm, turn her
double, inside-out, until she sees
  our faces looking down, waiting
for who's come back, to fold her in.

AMSTERDAM

—in memoriam Leo Lionni

He came at them with his stick,
   fending them off, sending them scurrying
down the long white corridor & out
   onto the green grounds beneath the
Tuscan hills. He had forgotten all
   his stories from all over.
His wife calmed him down, took his cane,
   got him back to bed, still raging,
but quieter. He turned to look for
   the hills, & as he did the mice
he'd whelped and weaned came out
   of their holes bringing him their
little wisdoms in wicker baskets,
   & he tasted each one & spat it out.
Bitter. Bitter. The mice scattered.
   He wanted to bite the hills, the
Chianti hills, take chunks out of them,
   leave teethmarks on Porcignano,
its boar-laden woods, the valley
   whose caves hid partisans.
But he lay back. He had heard
   canal water lapping at his feet,
the slap slap slap
   of oars under his window.
He gripped his stick and looked about
   for something to move.

THE PORCUPINE IN PORCIGNANO

—*in memoriam Leo Lionni*

In this air that's almost too clear
  is the charge that each dawn jolts the sun.
Each day is another dimension, like water.
  It takes you by surprise. I know nothing,
but can count on the visibly invisible
  here simple as a child's wish.
It calls, and these hills hear its voice groping upward
  until thunder grumbles through Chianti
corridors and the sky's a tinkling
  chandelier, swaying all afternoon.

As night falls the little scorpions
  on the kitchen walls are alert as dogs.
Things could go on forever like this.
  But then the storm breaks directly overhead,
as if right here, inside the farmhouse whose glass
  is poignant in flashes before slipping
onto the floor and shattering, whose bulbs
  go out on by one with glances at each other.
And then it's over, leaving a sky intermittent
  mauve. I look out the window. A porcupine
is crossing the road. Suddenly headlights
  shatter in it. Ball-lightning scuttles
into the dark and out the other side,
  becoming part of newly numinous night.

ALZHEIMER'S

"There we were promised a great, great life
and it waited, though we weren't yet born."
—Czeslaw Milosz

There at the window, returned from having lived,
   from the other end of the world, tiny people
falling into shape, each speaking a different tongue,
   each almost growing familiar, caught in the glass,
but
   I was afraid, drew the curtains,
pretended it was long ago when we were all
   at ease with each other, knowing who we were,
even if under it all we were just slaves to habit
   with our best clothes on,
                    until the yellow flower
filtered through the curtains, staining my face,
   so I remembered some of the names of this place
where I had grown accustomed to swampy streams
   and abandoned houses where dogs barked
as if they still lived here,
                & I started again
with a smell, not yet a memory, earth beginning
   to drink from tiny roots in my dark garden
against a sky growing darker & far off I thought I heard
   cries of seabirds like voices more durable than
the fractured fragrant world still reflected in me
   as the yellow flower folded again and through the window
I watched the night-sky where memory had no place
   & I covered my eyes to imitate the sky
have my mirror fill with emptiness & a flock of birds
   on the beach between the islands stood attentive
as ivory facing the lonely island scattered with
   holm oak & ivy which will never again be able
to hold onto a name as the changing tide keeps pushing in
   while it is asleep & when it is awake shines out
fresh and anonymous through leaf and trunk.

VARIATIONS ON THE FIRST ELEGY

—Wirf aus den Armen die Leere. . . .

A vase of ice, his dead wife's overshoes
   still outside where snow makes equal splendor
& the wind turns cobalt, tasting of bare rock.

Black soil had pushed up like a chafing of water
   & now is stiff waves. What sunlight's left
craves soft parts of the body, before dusk brings

new white weight, tightening things up, tying
   them down, burying more. Until some of the
small bones speak, a low murmuring deep in the body,

where the certain shape of death is formed. A shadow
   slips off the snow like a small rat. What
did our mothers tell us? And theirs?

Under the wind, rumblings of keels, encrustations,
   anagrams for darkness. But over all an errant music
starts to blow, radiating fruit like an orchard

not yet cut down, billowing bright lines like fruit
   not yet fallen. And a high humming begins in the skull
that's echoed in the pliant bones of birds,

in every nerve, as under a growing moon they twist
   in up and down drafts, shaping the air,
being shaped by the air, as he watches, and opens his arms.

WHITENESS

passing over, shredding
early dusk . . . Headlights approaching . . .

He's in a sailor suit, playing
in light snow.

Only a moment ago,
his cheeks were dusty with daisies.

Then one day, complicated quiet
with its disclaimers changed it all

into an old man who has dreamed
the same dream for three nights.

A child is pulling a sled.
The meal was interrupted.

Across the street, the doctor's blotchy hands
are picking the last blotchy apples.

They move in and out of the
whitening branches like needles.

Overhead, hidden stars tick-tock.
The hills too are drawing on their masks.

He has checked the world, then himself,
for relics of terror. He stops

by the gate to say nothing, leaving
black prints. Below, over the town,

orange lights form a memento like a fish-tail.
Headlights approaching . . . He looks for

the yellow bus and spits grit
from a passing car. The mountain

flies off the same way. He escapes
into the stones and the faint lawn.

The wind that brought him here
stirs uncertainty. There is nothing

between him and the child pulling
a sled. He cannot forget stories

that unwind like revenge. A child
is pulling an empty sled.

THE FROG PRINCE

Suicides don't always die.
  For some, each day the head wakes
not wanting to, to what's around
  as if through water
distorted, hands in shadows
  poring over them, hands
moving over and through
  everything, echoing themselves,
the way as a kid I tried to hold onto
  frogspawn that kept slipping
through my fingers, hoping it would
  come alive, but when it did, like a movie
monster, it was too much, and I
  dumped the lot down the drain.
When gone I missed them, went looking
  for more and woke screaming,
for now they twitched and swam
  in my head, trying to breathe
whatever there was to breathe,
  using it up.

WHERE THE WOODS BEGIN

My friend is now in dreams,
like the one where I rake a pile of hair
and leave it near the heaped-up grass.
Later, I scare myself so bad, I say:
"I thought the pile of hair a wolf!"
He's there to light it, turn fear
to smoke. And now his ash is planted,
though he wanted to be scattered on the water,
touch everywhere and everyone; those
he dreamed to being, believing the people
could be breathtaking, and Marx right.
His mother would have understood,
she who left her Russian Jewish home
and a husband who beat her when she read;
who joined the Party, washed office floors,
and in her early forties had this son
to a young Catholic priest from Ireland,
whose name she never told. She'd like it
that he lies scrupulously gray,
in an urn wrapped in brown paper,
placed in the last plot left
in the artists' cemetery, in the corner,
where the woods begin.

THE ROSE

"Rose, oh reiner Widerspruch . . ."
—RMR

My favorite poet was scratched by a rose
  while batting off the bees of the invisible.
I sit him down after he stumbles in from Brooklyn
  reeking of pitch and turpentine, which
reminds me of Randy Turpin (my favorite
  boxer) and Dick Turpin (no relation)
my favorite highwayman (and Black Bess
  his trusty steed). I'm thinking that I'm
not well. He doesn't look too hot either.
  Would you like some fruit? *Früchte?*
I ask. He is small, out of breath. It's
  all too much, he says (in German, natch).
I need a breather. And pretty soon there's
  pages of words floating in the air. A wind
gets up and whirls them around. I try
  to snatch some, grab one which turns out
to be an instruction manual in couplets.
  But it's beyond me. I don't know what
it's instructing. It could be anything,
  even how to write manuals. He is slightly
taller now, but still very slight. Modest
  to a fault, he says: I borrowed everything,
but I gave it back, rearranged a bit.
  Grab and grope. It's called—*Dasein?* I say.
Right, he says. It's all open-ended.
  Urgrund? Right again. Keep the doors open,
he adds. Then he keels over, transfigured,
  dying of blood-poisoning stuck again by a thorn
from the rose he plucked from the air to hand
  me to make his point, and which I dropped.

NERUDA IN PURGATORY

"Si me preguntáis de donde vengo, tengo que
conversar con cosas rotas . . ."

Blue patches of weather; shivered blue stone
　I try to scratch a fire from. A single swallow
balks where red water screeches & an invisible hand
　forces it into progressively narrower spaces.
Somewhere in the search for the useful,
　nuptial matter, there still may be flowers
to pluck from sleepy faces. But not here,
　the proletariat no more than a chronic itch;
not here where a man facing eternal loneliness
　can only shoot out words like pistons,
abandoning gears, staring at the Janus hood-ornament.
　I have been left to starve in a garden,
a jackdaw tacked to the gate, scarf fluttering
　in tacky red clods. I start a fire. Each spark
gropes upward, as if up was the only nourishment.
　They allow me my figurehead in the window
now the world is all shore. A sea-music less
　than half-roar takes up what it can.
I was wrong, I was right. I was left
　here where I devolve into spray, salt, bitter,
unlearned, not yet repentant. No one
　sees the blood in the sand I lay the driftwood over,
and light a match. *Hay tantos muertos . . .*

MAN ON THE MOON

—in memoriam E.T.

He marches, silent, from room to room as if we are divided
nations. I move my chair to avoid being run over. She continues
without paying him any attention. *And the Empress made me*
break it off. I gave him back the ring. He threw it in the river.
Silly woman, he said. Doesn't she know a man can be both?
Her grandfather glows in his shiny old suit like rotting wood.
He clumps around in brown boots polished to a high gleam,
round and round from room to room. Mishka follows,
yelping and nipping at his heels. On the table, remnants
of six places and a bottle of frozen vodka, half melted,
beads running down its sides. Once an admiral, now someone
with a hot star stuck under his tail so he cannot stop or sit.
But his eyes are fixed and quiet so maybe he is still sitting
in the gazebo, a Don Cossack parked outside, a little girl
on his knee. He sings out her name from time to time:
Elizabeth. He's pushing a hundred. The light from a crack
in the shutter strikes a wine glass and slices across the divan
and antimacassar and empty aspidistra bowl, touching
his features before clattering to the floor. He kicks out at Mishka
who, more surprised than hurt, sits down flat on his docked
spaniel butt. I lead the old man across the room and sit him down
at the table, where his legs keep working. Old Grandad.
California white wine. Vodka. It is a typical Sunday late afternoon
in July. They have all, except for him, gone back to the city.
You can see the sycamore outside the window start to relax,
the great boughs softened and still. It is still hot. When
will the sun explode? Soon, according to Elizabeth, now the moon
has left us. The old man has stood up and pulled on his cape,
the one with red silk lining, like a throat in tatters. Some walk
forever in God, some by the banks of the Dneiper. As tides
turn and buses run late he opens the door and takes off.
Moon's babies mewl like somebody down a well. Elizabeth
takes haddock from the freezer and drops it in the pan with
a crash. If she remembers to put water in and light the gas,
if she remembers not to fall asleep and let the cigarette fall
into her apron so she has to tell the firemen the smell

neighbors complained of was a nest of rats under her house,
   then all will be well. Through the front windows I watch
the admiral leave Savastopol with General Wrangel and take
   the orange bus to the Port Authority. I see them safely
back to 52nd Street and cousin Alexander's. Then I
   turn on the gas she's forgotten again, light it, fill the pan
and put it on the stove. Elizabeth is in her armchair, Moon
   and kittens on her lap, Mishka sulking at her feet. A Parliament
in one hand lets ash fall over her knees. A glass of something
   tilts in her other hand which she uses to point to the tape recorder.
It only has two speeds, fast forward and fast reverse. I shake
   my head. Once more we will not hear her husband's "The Plague"
or "Mary's Song," though once more Elizabeth tells me that
   this Mary is not the Mother of God but the loving whore,
and that although it is going to come, and it is going to come,
   she will never leave them. But the Pope is not happy.
From the kitchen he calls. He wanted cod. His white hairs clog the
   record player, so that too has not played in years, and she won't
let me replace anything. His face is scarred. He scratches a lot,
   and fights. "There's blood in my nails," she says. "My head itches.
Alexander in his imperious way says I should have him put down.
   Antique dealer! Seller of ancient pisspots! We Romanoffs are not
meant for death. We are survivors. Like Aunt Elizabeth, whose
   name they gave me. Have I told you the story of—." "Yes, many times."
"Don't interrupt, darling. The story of how soldiers threw her
   down a well, but peasants brought her bread? While she sang hymns.
When the White Army came they pulled her up and took away
   her body. It was immaculate and inoffensive, not even bruised,
though it had been in the water three months. It looked like marble.
   Her nurse took the body to Jerusalem and buried it. She said
the scent of roses oozed from the coffin. I have the wad of wool
   she wiped in it. Have you seen it? Where is it now? Perhaps
I gave it to Mountbatten. She was his aunt too. And a Sister of Mercy.
   And a saint. And where's her husband, Great Duke Serge?"
She paused to look around. "They killed him too," I said. "Yes,
   for helping Jews. I married one. Did I tell you how Maritain
converted him, and left us this house?" "Many times." "Blood
   in my hair? Hair in my hand? I used to bleed like a pig each month.
My life of blood. Do you remember when we watched a man walk
   on my moon? It was faked. Moon capsule! The moon's going

to blow up, and take us all with her, including grandfather, who
    doesn't want to go. Did I tell you of the time he went hunting—
what do you call those terrible big animals with horns?" "Buffalo."
    "Right. With Buffalo Bill. And they drank champagne. And my son,
you know I was married before. I told you about him. He ran away
    and joined the Foreign Legion and was never heard from again.
He is somewhere crying like a cat because he can't get home.
    I was only seventeen when I was engaged to the Grand Duke
Mirsky who pomaded his whiskers—not much younger than you
    so watch out for men like that. He also had nose hairs and boy-friends,
lots of them, all over Russia. It was a scandal after the Empress
    made me break it off. Nicodemus acknowledged the Lord,
like my dead husband whose music I can never hear again.
    Down, you voluptuous dog! Leave my wig alone! Darling,
get my wig will you? There, he's done it again. Leave the cat
    alone! They're not good for dogs. You know my sister—
of course you do. She was just here. She married a Dutch Mennonite
    who organized orgies and divorced her when she complained
of being alone and took to sleeping with her dog, a giant Alsatian.
    Now, I'm tired, darling. Tomorrow we'll review Russian
verbs of motion. Now when you go, lock the door. Moon,
    come here and bring your children. Last night I dreamed
of my dear husband for the first time since he died. We were in Paris,
    visiting museums and going to markets. We were very happy.
There was a full moon. After a while he told me he was ready
    to leave. I said I'd have to pack. Where we are going, he said,
we won't need baggage. But I must get money, I said. Nor money
    either, he said. Did I tell you there was a big full moon."

THE FIRE

The fire at nightfall unfurls, overwhelming,
  dumbfounding, its wings half-spread catching
the growing warmth, a taste for everything its fuel.
  Roaming deep inside is something reaching, roaming
like quicksilver, it pools, it boils, a whisper then a groan.
  The ax falling, the flower makes a great roar,
husks find words, the tide blazes and struggles to
  put itself out—oh, how the hawk tilts and loses
itself as I look through the conflagration to see
  the years catching up, roads petering out.
Here in the dark fire is just another form of darkness.
  It leaps, it falls, it drains, deforms. In its being
it is all reflection. That's you in the fire. In the flames'
  dark pools you can see your eyes, you can see
the sky in its poverty, its aftermath. The wheel turns
  a notch to unnerving night and you are beyond mourning.
Seamless, you unite your beginning to your end. You watch
  the fire as if it was your limbs crackling and splitting
like the northern lights as you lay on your back in a
  Minnesota lake, the heavens coming down, igniting
your body, the lake become the sky, the fires cooling
  as heaven flickered all round you, and all round
the collapsing sky consumed the lake consuming you.
  But now you drift, full of excuses and white flags,
trying to grasp the shadow you are, but how thin it is,
  how nebulous, how immune, as if you were in a circus
after the acts have left and what you're watching are old echoes
  of your own expectations there on the slack wire,
there in the numb lips and hesitant steps, while below the fire
  fumbles and falls, rears up to fill night's blank while coyotes
dip and quiver, focused, clarified, clarifying. The wind gets up
  and keeps everything calm. A chortle, a cough, a scream.
The lips go numb again. The throat clogs. Escape is not possible.
  Looking back, little flares come at you, lap at everything,
suck in what's left. It is fecund, it is plentiful, it is playful,
  it is everything, year to year. It has pursued you, like
the hound of heaven. It will find you, white flowers in its mouth.

AUTUMN ROAD

I live on Vega Mountain but still cannot
  find Vega for sure even though up here it's close—
as I look, the sky flaps like an open tent door
    or a sea where ships wait in a blossoming chaos,

crazed with trance. So I look for the ecstatic image
  here below where the year is dying fiercely,
releasing the sky's cold waters, each
    precise point inured and intenser the harder

I look. I pocket what I can and keep it like change.
  Tomorrow I will decide if I should think
everything ordained because it happened, if
    the charts are true, and how the world needs to

plunge back into the body to know what it means.
  Meanwhile the starry mesh tilts forward on its own,
squandering itself in renewal, fractured images glancing off
    themselves, glancing into visibility, each glance a spark,

expensive and slivery as fish beyond the fisher's reach,
  All flame and dancing darkness, wings of Blakean desire
that redeem and drown and redeem again
    the very air we breathe, and breathing change.

THE OHIO STATE UNIVERSITY PRESS/*THE JOURNAL*
AWARD IN POETRY

Spot in the Dark
Beth Gylys

Writing Letters for the Blind
Gary Fincke

Mechanical Cluster
Patty Seyburn

Magical Thinking
Joseph Duemer

Stone Sky Lifting
Lia Purpura

Captivity Narrative
Mary Ann Samyn

Blessings the Body Gave
Walt McDonald

Anatomy, Errata
Judith Hall

Crossing the Snow Bridge
Fatima Lim-Wilson

Popular Culture
Albert Goldbarth